TOUCH ANYWHERE TO BEGIN

TOUCH ANYWHERE TO BEGIN

JIM NASON

Clarise Foster, Editor

Cover design by Doowah Design.
Photo of Jim Nason by Don Smith.

This book was printed on Ancient Forest Friendly paper.
Printed and bound in Canada by Hignell Book Printing Inc.

"You Bring Yellow Tulips" was published on September 13, 2015, on-line in *HIV Here and Now: Poem-a-Day countdown to 35 years of AIDS*; "Waking" and "Winter's Underground" were published in *CV2*, Spring, 2014; "The Jade Hotel" was published in *The Gay and Lesbian Review* (Boston), April, 2015.

We acknowledge the support of The Canada Council for the Arts and the Manitoba Arts Council for our publishing program.

Library and Archives Canada Cataloguing in Publication

Nason, Jim, 1957-, author
Touch anywhere to begin / Jim Nason.

Poems.
ISBN 978-1-927426-85-2 (paperback)

I. Title.

PS8577.A74T68 2016 C811'.54 C2016-901627-7

Signature Editions
P.O. Box 206, RPO Corydon, Winnipeg, Manitoba, R3M 3S7
www.signature-editions.com

"...the tension between how we behave and how we are expected to behave."
— Carl Phillips

I. THE MANY-ARMED SHADOW

II. RAT OF MY DREAM

III GREEN NIPPLE

IV. SNOW LABYRINTH

I.

TOUCH ANYWHERE TO BEGIN

THE CORMORANT DRIED ITS WINGS ON A ROCK

"...there are openings in our lives
of which we know nothing."
—Jane Hirshfield

It stood like a black cross
on the morning lake. Goth gone Religion,
wings hanging off its bone-frame like a flag
or a warning, it was melancholy and joking. I walked
and thought about how the cormorants have killed all the trees
on the island. I walked and watched the unflinching bird.
My shadow trailing behind me, first round like a boulder,
then, long and thin, a good sized snake.

Too many omens for one day — a crow lands on the arm
of the chair beside me, breathtaking blackness and proximity.
Open heart, a Buddhist concept, a term that has come to mean
surgery. I thought I'd died and been transformed. The crow
was black silk to me — an invitation I was ready for — boldness
and stature, unwavering quiver, long-shadow nerve unfolding.

BLUE CANDELABRA

"...the tension between how we behave
and how we are expected to behave."
—Carl Phillips

Once, my friend Lisa, sober and naked,
placed a ladder on her bed, climbed up and brought a snake
down from the dusty attic. She named him Oscar.
She knew it was a him by the skin, she said, by the heft
and firmness, by the way the snake coiled around her chest
and how she was afraid, but held.

Always looking to the flaw in the mirror,
mistake on the typed page, weakness in my pushed
and stretched body — envy is a form of hatred,
the many-armed shadow, the flickering light
across my desk. I want to be fearless, the one
who climbs stark-naked to the ceiling, makes friends
with darkness, caresses the loveless snake
'til it sighs, then releases.

TRIGGERS

Thoughts like cars speeding between buildings.
Cone-shaped high-rises, dervishes spun from silver clouds.
Only an accident could slow things down, a pileup —
sequined donkeys, smoke-swirl, a hospital, an hypothesis,
a taxidermied wren — lifted from other poets poems.
Word traffic through my brain.

In Istanbul, after a heavy rain, we walked the Theodosian Walls, looked down the Well of Blood, witnessed torture chambers, the shady heart of the Seven Tower Fortress. In a field, four men around a dead horse. White bone of broken leg, its rolled-back eyes like milky moons. I was afraid of the brown, swollen belly; its long, flaccid penis picked at by flies, the wiry black tail no longer swatting them away. From the underworld, the vast field of mud, other words crawled in — cyclops, rat, death. The bullet hole in his forehead, a middle eye.

EDGEMERE

"...and what shoulder, & what art,
could twist the sinews of thy heart?"
—William Blake

I waited for you, for the scratch
and thump of you, for the cry of you
on the porch. For your bright eyes
and warmth I waited, but only heard wind
in the cedar, the repetitive sigh of waves. All night
I searched along sandy paths, calling your name,
calling you back. You limped toward the deepest dark.
I waited and looked up — in awe of how many stars
so many silent sparks. I waited for the sun
but it didn't rise, only spring haze and the waves.
In gold-brown silence, through darkness and sand,
you left. Burn, be the nighttime Tyger then. I'll wait
for you, your purr and tumble in the forest; retreating
waves each night, silver shadows of the breathing shore.

TOUCH ANYWHERE TO BEGIN

Many men came to the windowless room.
I was young, semi-conscious, drunk. The tentative
man touched my ankle, then calf. For the aggressive
one, for his leathery tongue, his knotted grip, I slept
and woke. I sat, rolled over, licked his black boot,
begged like a dog. A third man kissed me
lovingly, on the lips, and I cried.

Mastercard put up a pop-up
sales cave, an atmospheric detour off the subway path,
concrete floor seductive, blue neon dim. We came
by the thousands, the rush hour surge, through
Union Station — for texture and wonderment, the warm,
glowing screen. Touch Anywhere to Begin, it said.
Tap to Bobble. Swipe to Spin.

PRIZE READING

Your feet in those black shoes
are bigger than I thought they would be.
You are fine and handsome in your silver suit.
You've shaved your head and are tall, humble
as you stumble, then triumph, over your poem
about shivering foals and a willing slave.

Desire is a weed in the air as I walk today.
Not a dandelion, but its seed, a light floating
above me, a globe of white of cotton. The fact
of bare back and whip. How you made us
squirm in our red velvet seats. How I held
my breath, wanted more. When you finished,
applause throughout Koerner Hall — hands clapping,
palm slapping palm, skin against skin — *This too is love.**

*from "Snow Globe," Carl Phillips: *Silverchest*, 2013.

BLACK HORSE

If I bring you a fistful of bees
will you know their sting's true source?
If I add sweet grapes to the giving will you take them,
fill your mouth, conscious of biter seeds? If I feed you
a long silence will you taste the time-sealed tannin, lick
with your tongue its translucent skin?
Tonight, like no other, sex.

I live in a glass house at the edge
of a breathing ocean, windows submerged
by groaning waves. I see the underworld, the sand-salt
bottom, the tilt and swirl through current. I look up
at nighttime sea, black horse of my dream — moonlit,
foaming, its vast, ribbed underbelly, waves like
pounding thighs, me on my back beneath them.

TAB HUNTER'S HORSE

"Art is for the young. When you're old,
it's enough to look at a leaf."
— Richard Teleky

As we drive west a twister
of a thousand green keys, tree limbs shaking, your dog

Toby, spinning in the back seat, sunset like the curved back
of a cowboy tipping his ten-gallon hat.

Morning, now. Veined and creased as a finger in a hot bath,
the maple key's seed-end has heft, dark weight of earth; its

feathery body spun of oxygen and green. In last night's documentary,
the movie star cowboy said, When you get old,

there's nothing as good as shoveling manure, running your hand over
the rump and thigh of an unbridled horse. Sexuality at ease.

The wind-blown key — the same red-pink potential as an autumn
leaf — same veiny light of your finger tips. The heat devil along

St. Clair was sudden and otherworldly. Low-rumble thunder, summer
seized the city. Disembodied seeds, untethered to fate.

WHY IT'S EASY TO EROTICIZE THE DEATH-GORED MATADOR

Francis Bacon —triptych, 1987, oil on canvas

It's his gold-sequinned tights.
The rubies of his broad-shoulder stance.
His dusty hands gripping the scarlet muleta.
It's the taunt, the swish, his head held high.
The bullring drenched in blood.
The sword slicing into the bellowing
bull's back. It's the snort and thump,
the charge and gore between the crowd's roar.
It's the tender Minotaur, the laid-out man
on the marble table. His blood-crusted blouse.
The horn-slashed thigh. The suit of lights
snuffed out. Death stirred and rattled,
no stepping back, it's the pain
and red paint of the stretched grey canvas.

GEORGE DYER'S BACK

Francis Bacon — three studies of the male back,
triptych, 1970, oil on canvas

I.

There's a sensual thickness in your shoulders
and legs — your groin must smell of salt and sweat.
Your mauve-brown flesh is turning grey,
probably feels cooler now. In your right thigh
an invisible pocket for barbiturates.

II.

It's natural to sit naked in a barber's chair.
To be half shaved in the mirror. To have a massive,
well-muscled back, big legs and slicked hair.
To hold a razor in your shaking hand. To empty
your pockets of your craving self.

III.

Hung in a cage, the glassless mirror, a blue-black void
where your image should be. No half-shaved face
or chiselled jaw. Your shadow on the floor like the leg
of a chair — armless, headless, no rock-solid back down here.

NAGA BABA

Naga Baba's hair, orange and shagged
like a horse's tail. His eyes wet topaz
between a part in the bangs; lips parted, chapped
and powdered in ash. This photograph, taken
on your trip to Pushkar, is your gift to me.
Naga means naked. Sacred man, a strand
of beads brassy and worn, snakes around
his thick neck, his goatee matted
muddied; his chest, rough as football skin.
Tightrope of tensions; how much
did you pay him to pose? I asked. Did he smell
like weed? Was he steady as rock or yielding
like clay? Ashes and swelter, a questionable
loin cloth, how naked was he, I asked.

NIJINSKI

Toes pointed, arms raised, he dances
like a willing slave girl. Gold silk plié.
Twirl. Arms over ass
and legs, two men. A man
and a woman. A man rolling over
a woman and a man, I imagine myself
on the floor. Then, grand jete, across the stage.
War. Death. Confusion inside and outside
his head. Madness. At who?

We talk in bed about the performance.
You kiss my neck, each leg. To be that much
in the swell of the moment. To have
the drive, take those leaps — pointed toes
reaching fingers — to spread yourself that wide in the air.

DREAM

In the pecking order of dream weather
sleet and cold coequal. All night the insistent
tapping, the inside chatter, the 'he said
she said' of the day unleashed.
In and out of sleep, hovering over
images and words…
…out of my body and through the wall,
mind continues its clatter, the all night
trappings
of feral cats and hungry dogs
pink umbrellas, bladeless skates
silver keys and suntanned breasts
with pasty pink nipples…
metaphor on her knees … tugging at my head
on a blue-silk pillow
the day rewound and in colour.

II.

RAT OF MY DREAM

THE DESTINATION

I ran down an escalator and through
a well-lit shopping mall. Happiness lived
in my raised arms. My feet like wings.
I no longer needed sleep or food (although I would miss
green curries and red grapes), nor any of the tougher emotions
that built up my chest and legs. Bodily functions, in general,
had become redundant. I flew past the public library,
daubed away a residual tear, the memory of a four day flu.
My destination was clear but I could not place my finger
on its glass throat. The pulse of her perfumed arm
across my shoulder. Swirls of morning light
against the bedroom window.
I could still hear the doors singing
when my eyes opened to the snow.

CITY WITH ANIMALS

Max Ernst — oil on canvas, 1919: 66.6 x 62.2 cm

I.

HOME

Blurred neon, April snow pink
and gold along York Street, down
to the silver lake. Silence and Max
on my wall — O! to be omnipotent, to hold
a boar-bristle Swenson like his. Mauve
nostrils on a red-brown cow; green horse;
tumbling albatross; the moon eclipsed
like a black dot; the cow looking back
with amber eyes, natural for her
to watch you from some grassy knoll
adjacent to a distraught woman
in green and black. Morning light
against my window, ice
like milk frozen on glass.

II.

SEX

One billion transformations
in the body per second — stem cells
differentiating, omnipotential
to unipotential — the heart cell
different from the bone marrow
cell, different from the red blood
cell, different from eyelash
or pupil. Naked, I light candles,
surround my body with flicker;
the keyboard where I type red, pink,
and blue-sentiment poems. Early spring,
the nocturnal prism; brown curves, pale green
strokes, Ernst's mythic cow — ears alert,
nostrils flared, eyes alive with flame.

III.

CHAOS

One light flickered
off and then another; morning sky
monotone, falling, coarse as canvas
without paint. Daylight shatters
my desk. Candles like hope, memory
of you leaning over the bed, me
learning it's better to give than receive
and then AIDS. Micky, Bruce and Donny
and the famous guys like Foucault
and Haring die while the world
gets hung up on their naiveté
about Rock Hudson; cracked bible
and lacquered hair, Anita Bryant pounding
the last nail into Robert Mapplethorpe's coffin.

IV.

STILL LIFE

It wasn't his sexualized lilies
or the vase of limp tulips, gorgeously phallic
in their mauve demise, it was the black guy
with the bullwhip, the explicitness of this,
the rough-trade beauty of the photograph
that caused the stir. Now, the continuum
of tyranny in August: Osage County — Meryl,
mother of girls, matriarch in the patriarchal dust.
Pill-poppin' story-swappin', everyone gone south,
Julia Roberts with dirt in her gold-brown eyes.
If we could see into the future, we'd never get out
of bed, she says, as she leaves Ewan McGregor
sleeping, a marigold breeze, flowered curtains
fluttering above his bearded face.

V.

PAINT

A dreamlike idea
of green castles, narrow streets,
faceless men, tired women; the soul
of a cow personified by her curled forelock,
eyelashes above flashy eyes, curved nostrils
fleshy as Marilyn in mauve-girdled light. Ghost
of a rearing horse, falling albatross, the up side
of bristle, a vision that never was but always is,
born of place and genes — seamless
horizon from my window — city and lake,
waves unthawing like sludgy pewter, morning
sun a wedge of light under rearing clouds,
you in the kitchen shouting: The cat
kept me awake all night.

VI.

ANIMAL

Mauve as a renaissance landscape,
clouds over the thawing lake
building like bruised biceps
I saw once at a dirty gym. Omnipotential
to unipotential— conspicuously sexed,
the cervix looks like the head
of an erect penis. I want to stay
in these six sonnets, stacked
in exhibition frames; the cat asking
to be fed; glossy image of a virus
in the Globe and Mail; Max Ernst
on the wall; you in the kitchen, hands
in hot water rinsing glass. It's your turn,
you shout. It's your turn to feed the cat.

WAKING

The clock falls back and the cat
doesn't give a damn about the hour.
She howls at five and five-ten; she howls again
at five-twenty and six. She knows there's no heft
in my silencing voice. Daybreak grit under my feet,
I trip through gauzy dark, bend to feed her as night
backs into gutters and lanes: feral, silent.
The rat of my dream, low to the ground,
had a brown tail the length of a garden snake.
I could smell its breath, the grass-like sweetness.
I touched its feet, a dozen white spiders
crawled across my fingers, birth sac
of light cut free.

CRANES

Night opens into day sky.
Roads muddy and widen while cement trucks queue
back-to-front like rumbling tanks. Construction workers
dominate downtown food-courts; dusty and rough
they sit among the pearls and ties. The Ritz, Trump,
Four Seasons…one hundred and fifty towers
shoot up. I'm not afraid to walk under
swinging cranes as they hoist steel girders, bent
and dangling. Vats of cement, sheets of glass, I marvel
as they are hoisted, watch from the ground
as they swing over streets, sidewalks, even
the expressway. I think about the people
who will live on the 78th floor. Wonder who
would nest in the shifting sky?

FOUR MINUTES, THIRTY-THREE SECONDS

"There is no such thing
as silence."
—John Cage

A car door slams.
An engine starts.
In the crowded parlour, Ruth
hits the nothing note.

Her back is straight. Her skin pink
with the blush of the concert.

She paces down
the silence, her fingers poised
above the keys.

I clear my throat.
Someone drops
a pen or a pencil.

She lifts and closes the piano lid.
Turns another page.

No music in the room
but music.

We listen.
Hear each note where there are none.

October gold — branch of maple —
the shimmering glass door has opened.

WINTER'S UNDERGROUND

People I don't know
but with whom I shuffle
through the 8:45 corridor.
Weaving winter's underground,
someone's briefcase bumps my knee;
someone else's red backpack
close to my chin. A broad-shouldered man
smelling of damp wool and musky cologne.
I wrestle the shadow of a grey coat. This morning
I couldn't bear the weight of the cat. Lifting her
from my lap, placing her on the kitchen floor,
head-bowed, she did not move, staring
down rejection. Not having words
for please or love.

UNDER THE EXPRESSWAY

The mournful hum of building traffic.
Infinity shifting its morning shadows.
I try to receive the day with grace, slowly
take in the cold air, step over a wide
sheet of ice. A worker hammers a pipe —
a tiny clang clang clang like a schoolyard flag pole.
In childhood's spring there's a patch of ice,
a small puddle glazed with snow crystal.
You pound it with your heel, trying
to break through — for the sound
of the cracking, the pleasure
and power in your brown-buckle boots.
For the splash above water — the just right
pressure to bring the stuck puddle to life.

OPENINGS

You spend five dollars for a single coffee
but don't give the homeless man change.

Digital seconds count down
the crosswalk; then, the solid red hand.

You wait at the intersection —
Drain City scribed on the side
of a plumber's truck;
Royal Taxi without a passenger;
Wheel-Trans speeding past.

You lean toward your day —
the tour bus idling exhaust;
tall buildings shimmer gold and silver;
the questions you will be asked but cannot answer.

Some of these you will love; hold those close
to your sad heart. Regret's cup
held up for change.

You step off the sidewalk, instructed
by the light.

OFF RAMP

One car at a time against the backdrop
city, sunrise light in your eyes. The off ramp
circles a cloister of lawn and maples; two red
Muskoka chairs in the center, chained
there, big-arm empty.

Brake lights, horns and the ringing
bell of the ferry arriving in York Pier.
Construction everywhere — in the gravel
triangle that was the police impound lot,
in the narrow strip of concrete between the expressway,
skyscraper A and skyscraper C. Yield to the circle you say
to yourself, as you look down at the side- by- side pair
bridged by chain and need. Yield to the circle.
Pray to the last patch of green.

FALL

Splintered light through blue-black cloud, October
gust of trash across Church Street. The teenage boy
in Dollar Store makeup, one red high-heel on his foot,
the other a begging cup. What city god brought him
to this corner, sat him between a growling pit-bull
and a girl with a pierced eyelid? She'll go blind
I think. Then I see the white cane and empty stare.
Her eyes are milky against her white skin; she raises
her face but does not squint at the sun dividing cloud.
Her life must be the life of heightened smells —
cigarette smoke, car exhaust, marijuana, the dog's
musky coat? To not see is to tilt into every sound —
the growling dog, cutting wind, the shivering boy
taking coin from his high-heel cup.

CITY BEACH

The blue car, covered in frost turns silver; ice
mixed with sand-grit collides with the quay. Sky
is flat and a bit of grass this side of the harbour
has turned white again; one foot anchored in December,
April does not smell of sex or spring-stirred mud. Thin
shadows of lampposts tethered to sidewalks, sun strikes
the backs of skyscrapers; stunned and tired, geese have
returned, a zigzagged V. Last fall's colours made us
sing gold and orange. We ate more, grew distant
with evenings, spent our time in subways and movies.
Cool mornings, we walked the edge of the dock
with caution; stepped over droppings left by the geese.
The lake seemed unstoppable, insistent wind-chopped
waves pushed us over, frosted our hair silver-grey.

ENOUGH

Chain of people linked on a journey.
All of us together, rushing forward, rain
on the roof of the train, flooding Rosedale Station.
Migration from one stop to the next, slant
standing, we lean into the tunnel
as if we could will the train to fly
over whatever caused its sudden stop.

One life is not more than another.
I push through the crowd, look down
on the track at the woman's coat lifting
in a breeze caused by the northbound train,
its flickering shadow on the track, relief
or grief, a great black bear torn
by its merciful self in half.

RELAPSE

Morning has diminished the steamy glass,
the bathroom mirror more tarnished than the night
before. I mull over my dream of an enormous
white snake, his strength wrapped around my legs,
how I was afraid of being strangled by his rough
speech, sexual slur. In another life I was a rat
(still hard for me to say), running parallel
with blood-orange walls, flattening under
baseboards, fearing that the bread I had eaten
was tainted. Shadow frightens me —
I prefer direct light, openings bright
as a hospital birth. I lather my face
in the steamy mirror, scrape the blade across
my rough chin, shoulder the glow of unmet days.

THREE SEVENTY

The vacuous sigh of jackhammered stars
disappearing one by one and the suck and grunt of mud
being tossed from the watery pit of the construction site.
Iron beams chained and hoisted across night-sky yield
and sway. Side-by-side, through hard-hat rain, two workers
carry grey-white sheets of drywall between them. Halogen
light for the overnight shift through the window, I close
the curtain, click off the sea-bent news.

Dream-tilt head hanging over the edge,
legs spread and gripping, I reach under
the bed — dust balls, a pair of men's white boxers,
a rolled off sock in an knot, the black pen I'd lost;
a metaphysical, protracted thought — the aircraft
slid into the ocean and no one saw.

HUNGER

Hunger is a starving dog
in a back alley. You know its misery
by rib and spine, through its sodden
black coat. The monarchs have gone
to Michoacan, migrated back to the sanctuary.
Inexplicable flight through rain, cold
and wind, instinct unfolding.

Afternoon sky optimistically blue,
the monarchs have returned— one near
the off ramp of the expressway, another
landing on a thin branch of backyard forsythia;
in the laneway behind the falling down garage
— weightless, buoyant, the martyr submits
to the dry, cracked mouth of a barking ghost.

HONEST

"…sighing and fidgeting in an unmoving line."
— Laura Kasischke

Looking for shade on the exposed
balcony, residual overnight, cool mingling
with warm air. Garbage floating up from the bin —
blood-stenched, dappled light of last night's dream
of me naked with two men in back-alley Tangiers.

Afternoon jog with my shirt off, pretending
I don't care — my body sagging
incandescent, dripping. Afterglow
on the reddish bark of June maples. Later, a nap
among the many-shaped geraniums, slant shadow
of the high-rise next door slicing the terrace in half.
Plantar fasciitis, cramps in my calves and my back
turned to stone. All that running.
All the running through streets, and fear.

VOLTA

This wound up darkness stirs
the poplars, peppers the concrete, greens the green
of cedar, butters the yellow porch gold.
                    I've waited for your warm hand
on my shoulder, for your body, callous and curved
like a C against me, for your arrival at the party
where I strengthened the fire. I waited for you
to fill the velvet seat at the midnight movie, to be
the night-walk from the tedious job, the enigmatic
stranger in tight white pants on the southbound train;
                    red-gold September in the aged-hard
maple; the icy glaze of December on the concrete walk;
April-wet crocus in silvery grass; the hot summer day,
slap-happy feet, of August rain on a steamy roof.

EARLY MORNING

A barge crosses the lake
and I think it's on fire.
Only the reflection of the rising sun
shooting across its cargo. These trees
along the water's edge have turned
red. A jogger runs beneath
their sprawling glow. How did I get to this
place above the city pier? This coveted
apartment with more rooms than plants.

A boat on fire.
The jogger in his fluorescent sweatshirt.
Sun flashing across subtle waves.
As if I could possibly hold this
transient rising. As if it were ever mine to own.

TYLER

Wires collapse, the house goes dark;
no person to navigate the ice with us.
My nephew exhales cold air, says he hallucinates.
Sad with answers and splendid brown eyes, he knows why
he was born and is fine with the weight of that. Not from god
like god in grandma's bible — creation comes from semi-visible
pyramids in his dreams, neither sand nor air. I meditate,
he says. My body is not my body, green- blue waves
float out from my chest. I look up, want to hold him,
but can't, the god of shyness owns me, the god of reason
judging. He says, sometimes you're my poet uncle,
a giant white bird with gold beak and brass claws,
sometimes you're the bald guy
throwing salt on the slippery steps.

III.

GREEN NIPPLE

DISAPPEARING

I imagined the strange objects
that various letters could manifest. It started off
innocent enough — A for bad apple; B for funeral bier.
When I got to W, I felt the weight of a glass heart
on my chest, cobalt unlike any blue I've ever seen: in its center,
my father in his uniform, standing at ease. W is for William,
I decided. Further along the highway a white-out, wind
and swirling light, the disappearing lane and uncertainty.
Then, the wide sky and frozen fields, blue and gold
like a Van Gogh; the cold, sunny drive and at the far end
of afternoon the funeral parlour's parking lot — snow piled
and edged, a perfectly ploughed rectangle of grief;
a pitchfork for scattering straw over ice, its worn wooden
handle, the W of it stuck into a stately mound of white.

WHAT REMAINS

I want winter to end.
I want it to stay.
Snow falling, flakes of night.
Colourful spines side by side: new
books. The orange and gold carpet
he brought from Morocco.
In the antique vase, neglected tulips'
red-yellow demise. And so morning
unfolds again. The brown hardwood
turning crimson. Grief expanding.
Pick up my pencil. I dare you, try.
Speak with compassion
when dismissing winter. Before
the rains of April, the need to unravel
all the good coldness has done. Light
like this, the complexity of it.

TISSUE

The train slides into the station,
the day expands — Bienvenue à Montréal.
Litter along rue Dorchester stuck in frozen
heaps — newspaper, soda can, a cigarette
package with cancerous lungs faded grey.
I walk the edge of the river, marvel
at its violent thawing, take photos
of silver saints. We all leave
our bodies at some point. I imagine
the journey mine might make — first
the quiet departure from porous skin.
Disorientation. Then, clarity.
No grief, just release. Death is
an unthawed tissue floating in April wind.

VASE

In the Bardo, spirits sidestep
one another, bow or else look away
to some black-on-grey horizon.
My father dead is more of a boy
than the soldier he was alive.
Mommy, he cries, his hand reaching up
to strangers pushing by.

But he wasn't a Buddhist or, for that matter,
a very good Catholic. His ashes in the urn
all the truth that's left.

It's easy to remember him living
in Montréal. Stand straight. Shoulders back.
He marched through rue Dorchester on fire.
He carried a plastic bag
that looked heavy, set it down
on the table between us.
It's hand-painted, he said, proud.

The orchid more alive
in that vase than any other —
brilliant white, crimson-streaked throat
opened wide, cut stems drinking
clear water, the flower reaching up
through a crack in the curtain.

° ° °

A silver crane flew across
the haze of my dream. Its dangling legs
slashed the caesarian sky.

My sister painted crows
and women with red flowers.
Orange peonies, handfuls of tissue
like orchids fell from the porcelain sky.

WOLVES

The orchid budding in a vase
on my father's desk.
My funeral shirt hung
like a dead man
on the back of the door.

I know who I am
and then I don't. Fuzziness about
today's eulogy. What to say to the expectant crowd?
What words for the sad, angry faces?

How pathetic the man who leaves his children
to the wolves.

My heart like a too tight shoe.
Speak with respect to what is passing.

This world you are leaving…

A small green nipple foreshadows
the orchid flower. Soon, a curved white tongue
tipped to the sky; creases along pink petals
like puckered skin, inside the mouth,
red-mauve stain.

How does the flower know where it's going?

There is nothing we do that is without meaning —
step lightly when waking the dark,
vaults within vaults.

The world you are leaving will persist.

STAIN

I swim so far out the shoreline disappears.
I fall so fast I become invisible.

His children are here and some of their spouses;
his grandchildren too, the ones allowed to come.
A preacher gives a careful sermon. Wine
and coffee stains blotch the powder blue
carpet; row after row of vacant pews.

I get to my feet, speak
words I've typed onto the page.
Compassion has a vivid imagination —
salutes and trumpets, a grand chapel
filled to capacity with mournful people,
his gold-wing casket floating above the cobblestone road.

EULOGY, CEDAR AND RAT

Handfuls of cedar, cluster of unlit candles,
I'm a fool for evoking ghosts. Ghost of the dead
deer hit by a hill-bound car, the injured owl outsmarted
by the hungry fox, the rat that crawled into the dark
beneath my bed once the harm was done. Ghost
as guide. Ghost as tormentor. When the sun rises,
a thousand ice caskets float en masse to the center
of the lake for the final thaw, soon to return as light-tipped
waves. In my hand, the cedar twig, tugged from a cluster
of shrubs, damp from snow I shook off. Speak to me
of winters past and the winters before that; uncountable
stars suspended in deep black. Speak, I say, as I strike
the match. Speak, I beg — the teary-eyed owl
and sated red fox, the thick bellied rat of my father.

HEFT OF THE BUNDLE

Spring to summer, green to grisâtre,
the crisp stalks of asparagus went limp.
Pointed tips collapsed but you ate them.
For the smell of green in your urine
the next morning. For the promise
of happiness when you bought them.
The walk to the market in the rain, you
choose them above all others. The heft
of the bundle, halted tips, tiny flowers
about to explode. The moment they were
cut down evenly captured. Salt, oil
and pepper, too much steam ruined them —
stringy, green in your teeth.
You don't know who to blame.

IV.
SNOW LABYRINTH

UPPER EAST SIDE

for Philip Seymour Hoffman

There's a snowy kind of Sunday light
in the room; snow tracing the black limbs
of skeletal maple, falling across windshields glazed
with February ice. In the morning paper, a photograph
of Phil's daughter, seven years old, hanging on
to Mimi O'Donnell's sleeve — worried, petrified, she
looks as if there's no place to fall with her grief. I marched
through a snow labyrinth, stomped a path, stopped to pet a lion
and then a white tiger; at the end, a leviathan snowball, snake
slithered up its curve; I was afraid, not of dying, but of its teeth,
the pinch like a staple remover, hooked under my skin. The hearse
moved through the city, like a polar bear on ice — strong, steady,
stopping now and then — morning snow smells of ice
and oblation, lights the grey light of Broadway dimmed.

CLOSING MONOLOGUE

"Only one step and my deep misery
would be beatitude."
— *Rainer Maria Rilke*

Under stars, January's icy candles, the Staten Island ferry
pushing through dark. Spalding Gray in the cold salty spray
and punch of waves. Breast stroke. Gasp. Stroke. Manhattan's
staggered backdrop, silent blocks too far for him to reach. Above,
a solitary helicopter, circling Liberty's wind-slashed flame. Gasp,
stroke, tide and undertow in sync, the underbelly of his closing
monologue. More things move than blood in the heart.

Later, one witness said she saw a dolphin
tipped on the crest of a surging wave. Another said he slid
into the water like a sleepy child between soft grey sheets.
Some say it was the car accident. Others agree it was
the father-son movie, the selling of the house, the genetic
stitch of his mother's suicide. Gasp, stroke, pitiless waves,
the ocean darker than any stage. He must have been terrified.
Of death, the trembling chopper hovering above, the amber light
above the blackened door. They pulled his body from
the East River, early spring thaw, first loose grasp of March.

WHAT I HEARD IN THE WEST VILLAGE

Desire and longing clenched in a stretch
along the back of my throat. My eyes
water too— April, pink blossoms along
sun-lit West Tenth, snow on a cluster
of yellow tulips. A man with a microphone
in front of a red truck, but not a fire truck; a fireman
with a scorched helmet in his enormous hand.
When the snow stopped and the smoke
we moved closer. There was bright light
and silence. The wind was no longer
stirring, there was a flood from the gold pump,
flickering on the ice-glazed sidewalk. Flames
rolled across the roof. Windows darkened.
The fire wouldn't die for the snow, he said.

THE JADE HOTEL

Sober and somber but still the same
I sat in a bar surrounded by travelers with tablets
and iphones, wrote on white paper with a sharp pencil,
felt old and it rained enough to make me less lonely.
There were black and white photographs hung above
red-velvet booths. Music fell from the ceiling — Antony
singing If It Be Your Will. I wrote to the tap tap tap
against beveled glass, went for a walk with a red umbrella
to the West Village. White blossoms filled trees along Sixth.
A woman with a paintbrush holding up her blonde hair
planted daffodils in small black pots down the side of her
concrete walk-up. I drank coffee at Jack's on Tenth,
listened to jazz and rain, various wet couples
held hands at tables. It all started again.

THAW

for John Ashbery

Clouds throw inky dashes to the ground
while we sit in a circle and whisper
dark rhymes, scribe tentative truths
into the half-awake earth. Dear One,
all the thin wolves in the ravine
are talking about you, howling
coarse curses. Did you hear the rolling
thunder, see rose-coloured light slashing
across the pot holes? Overnight, buds shot
out like bouquets on winter-thin branches,
back-knifed dawn with words. Feather
the sparrow's cry into ribbons. Mop
the moment. The river is running
girls in pink shoes.

YOU BRING YELLOW TULIPS

I.

James Schuyler, master of azalea,
rose and hyacinth, wrote an elegy
for Frank O'Hara, who stopped breathing
the blues on the New York City afternoon
Lady Day whispered her last note
and died.
Michael Cunnigham wrote a novel
about Virginia Woolf after her suicide in Sussex
where three grey sparrows held court
on a branch of Field Maple
and a green-brown bomber
shot across a rain- streaked English sky.
Mark Doty wrote a poem
about Michael Cunningham
writing on Virginia Woolf and the Bleeker Street
flower shop where Mrs. Dalloway, but not the real
Mrs. Dalloway, said she would buy the flowers herself.

II.

Meryl Streep in sunglasses
walking down a Manhattan street
through what appears to be
snow, arms heavy with forsythia,
hydrangea and roses, enters a tumble-down
building, looks out a window where glass should be.
A decrepit elevator takes her up
through the graffitied core of a warehouse.
The rattling gate opens onto a dying-from-AIDS
poet, she steps into his loft apartment, seems to be
holding her breath while simultaneously talking, as only
Meryl Streep can. She places the flowers
in two vases — blue hydrangeas in one,
yellow roses in the other, and picks trash
off the kitchen floor.

III.

You bring yellow tulips
when you come for dinner. Yellow tulips
in January! I say. You also bring Macon Village,
your crazy down-east accent and I pretend
not to see bruising, blotches like blue-white flowers
on your chin and cheek, how you struggle
to swallow your night time antiretroviral
with a gulp from your glass
of red wine.

IV.

In the movie, Mrs. Dalloway
is in love with the dying poet.
She misses her youth, longs for
that first kiss, the promise
of a single perfect day. Now this
slow and confusing death, the poet's suicide
tumble from a flung open window — sadly
beautiful with its gently- falling- snow effects.

V.

Bessie, Billie — enough of the blues,
sad as a marigold's stench, you say. Let's watch
that movie again, the one with red roses
in every unhappy vase. Where Meryl melts
down in the end, with a single mauve orchid
on the window ledge, reaching
like Lady Liberty, for the moon
or is it Mars? up there
among satellites, stars like cinquefoil —
silver-blue flowers, étincellant.

FATHER'S DAY, THIRTEENTH AVENUE

Christopher's eyes (black as his hair) shine in end-of-day
sun. 100 degrees, New York, all the others have left. We sit
on the steps outside The Center. Mosquitos bite my back
and neck. We talk about addiction and Father's Day, *admitted*
we were powerless… A breeze makes me glad to be in my body.
Christopher reaches into his shorts. At first, I don't look.
His underwear is red, the black band reads: American Shark. It's hard
not to notice his skateboarder's butt and legs. The elastic snaps
when he pulls out his iphone. Where I come from, he says, pointing
to the phone, guys don't draw. Black and white monsters, a ramshackle
house; one drawing in colour, a fishbowl with pink goldfish. I lean
closer, ask if I can touch the screen, enlarge the art. Yes, he says.
I touch it — coax it. He leans back, sighs. My father hates me,
he says. My mother is dead. We sit for a long time. The concrete
wall radiates. He tells me he is lonely, doesn't want to go back
to Brooklyn. His honesty is fire against the slow-moving dark.
His mouth is fire. His legs are fire and iron. *We came to believe*
a power greater than us could restore us to sanity…
What's your story? he asks. Empathy beyond his youth.
Unsolicited. Uninhibited. Who hurt you? he says, reaching…
his finger nudging the top-secret spot, under my second rib.
Small bruise on his knee, cuts on his elbow and wrist.

SEVEN DOORS

"The restless choir
that any human life can be… "
— *Carl Phillips*

Seven doors in this apartment — each with a glass
knob to touch, turn, adore — an entrance or exit,
opportunity or loss, risk or redemption. Tonight
Obama proclaimed revenge on ISIS, but didn't
call it that; our mayor announced a tumour
in his stomach, larger than a bullet, not
a blood orange. This room opens, beyond
the late news, the bed where you sleep
coiled against me. I turn off the television,
stare up at darkness, wonder about planets
beyond my reach. Someone put glass
on the mahogany doors. I watch you breathe in
and out, moonlight in a square on your exposed
shoulder, sturdy and translucent as crystal.

NOTES ON POEMS

Blue Candelabra
Carl Phillips' quote is from the *Globe and Mail* interview: May 31, 2014.

Triggers
A number of phrases in this poem are borrowed from other poets: "sequined donkeys" is from Jan Conn's "Touch Me Anywhere to Begin: A Biography of Eva Peron"; "smoke-swirl" is from Mark Doty's "Deep Lane" in *Deep Lane Poems*; "a hospital, an hypothesis" is from Lisa Robertson's "Cinema of the Present" in *Cinema of the Present*; "a taxidermied wren" is from Henri Cole's "Free Dirt" in *Nothing to Declare Poems.*

Three Seventy
"Three Seventy" refers to the flight number of the missing Malaysian Airlines aircraft that disappeared, never to be seen again.

Honest
Laura Kasichke's quote is from "Memory of Grief" in *Space in Chains.*

Tab Hunter's Horse
Richard Teleky's quote is from his novel *Winter in Hollywood.*

Seven Doors
Carl Phillips' quote, "The restless choir /that any human life can be," is from *Double Shadow Poems.*

Closing Monologue
The father-son movie referred to is Tim Burton's movie *Big Fish* — the movie that Spalding Gray had seen the night he jumped from the Staten Island Ferry. The poem was inspired by Daniel MacIvor's play *Who Killed Spalding Gray?* The Rilke quote is from *The Notebooks of Malte Laurids Brigge.* The line about the heart is from "Night" in *The Blue Estuaries* by Louise Bogan.